ORDINARY TWINS
Momma, What is CoronaVirus?

Written By
Jacquiline Hamilton

Illustrated By
Sidra Mehmood

"Momma, we are missing school and we miss all our friends too! When can we go back to school?" ask the boys.

"I am sorry guys, school is closed because there is a bad virus called Coronavirus going round that is making people very sick," explains Momma.

“What is Coronavirus?” asks Lachlan.

“Coronavirus is an illness that can spread from one friend to another when they play together if one of them has the virus,” replies Momma.

SOCIAL
DISTANCING

"So, we need to do something new called social distancing," says Momma.

"What is social distancing?"
asks Braedan.

"It means keeping space between yourself and other people. This might mean we have to spend more time at home for now," says Momma.

HIGH FEVER
HEADACHE
RUNNY NOSE
SORE THROAT
COUGH

"It's so boring at home, we want to go and play in the park with all of our friends Momma!" yells Braedan.

"I wish you could but if one of your friends is sick and you get sick you will need to go to hospital. You might end up with a fever, a cough, a sore throat and feel very tired," explains Momma.

"Remember not to touch your face," says Daddy.

"Why can't I touch my face?" asks Braedan.

"That is because this virus can get into our bodies through our eyes, noses and mouths," says Daddy.

"Can the doctor make people better?" asks Lachlan.

"'The Doctor can fix some people but unfortunately there are some people that the Doctor can't fix. We can avoid getting sick by social distancing," says Momma.

"I don't like wearing a mask Daddy!" exclaims Braedan.

"A mask will help protect you and others from getting sick. See Momma and Daddy are also wearing masks when we go out in public," says Daddy.

C
B
A

"Washing our hands can also keep us safe.

"Let's sing the ABC song while we wash our hands with soap and water to make sure we kill all the germs.

"If there is no water, we can use hand sanitizer to disinfect our hands after touching objects," says Momma.

"Guys, it's homework time. Even if school is closed we still need to do our homework," says Momma.

"It's Braedan's turn first," argues Lachlan.

"I don't like homework!" cries Braedan.

"The quicker we finish, the quicker we can play again," says Momma encouragingly.

"OK, homework is finished, well done boys!" praises Momma.

"Now let's give Daddy some space as he is working from home today.

"Can you please keep quiet, Daddy is in an online meeting on his computer," Momma warns.

"Daddy is working from home because many companies, big and small, also need to keep their staff safe and to help not spread the virus," explains Momma.

WASH YOUR HANDS
WEAR A MASK
SNEEZE INTO YOUR FOREARM OR ELBOW

"We are slowly getting back to normal. Momma and Daddy will go back to work soon and the schools will open again too.

"When you get back to school you need to be careful in class and in the playground. Wash your hands often, wear your mask and if you sneeze or cough do it into your elbow.

"It's important to have fun with your friends, but it's also important to stay safe," Momma explains to the boys gently.

GOOD
NIGHT

"Night night my loves! You both did very well at social distancing today.

"You helped keep lots of people safe including yourselves and Momma and Daddy.

"I am very proud of you!" says Momma.

Jacquiline Hamilton and her husband Graham live in Hong Kong with their twin boys Braedan and Lachlan. She manages her salon, Aphrodite Hair and Makeup, where she provides a space of comfort and relaxation for her clients. Jacqui wrote and self-published the Sai Kung Police Officers in 2018, her first kids book featuring her adorable twins as characters.

She recently took up poetry as a way to release tension, and to uplift and inspire herself through life's journey. In 2019, Jacqui published A Walk Through Healing, a collection of her poetry.